From
CATERPILLAR
to
BUTTERFLY

Camilla de la Bédoyère

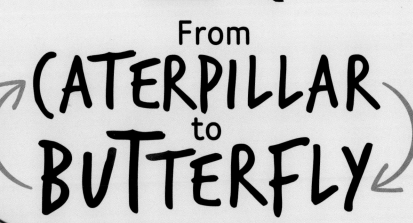

Quarto is the authority on a wide range of topics.

Quarto educates, entertains and enriches the lives of our readers—enthusiasts and lovers of hands-on living.

www.quartoknows.com

Words in **bold** are explained in the glossary on page 22.

© 2019 Quarto Publishing plc

First published in 2019 by QED Publishing,
an imprint of The Quarto Group.
The Old Brewery, 6 Blundell Street,
London N7 9BH, United Kingdom.
T (0)20 7700 6700 F (0)20 7700 8066
www.QuartoKnows.com

A catalogue record for this book is available from the British Library.

ISBN 978-1-78603-614-8

Manufactured in Guangdong, China PP062019

9 8 7 6 5 4 3 2

MIX
Paper from
responsible sources
FSC® C001701
www.fsc.org

Picture credits
(t=top, b=bottom, l=left, r=right, c=centre, fc=front cover, bc=back cover)

Corbis
17t Darrell Gulin, 20l Danny Lehman
Getty Images
13b Kim Taylor & Jane Burton, 16-17 Darrell Gulin
NHPA/Photoshot
10l Kitchin & V Hurst, 10t Kitchin & V Hurst
Photolibrary Group
1b Wally Eberhart, 18 Don Johnston, 20–21 Radius Images
Science Photo Library
3, 22t Dr John Brackenbury
Shutterstock
fc chockdee Romkaew, 2t Willem Dijkstra, 4c Peter Schwarz, 4tr Ambient Ideas, 5c ehtesham, 6cr Ron Rowan Photography, 6 cb Breck P. Kent, 7ct arka38, 7 rc Leena Robinson, 8lb Leena Robinson, 10b Kathy Keifer, 10c bhathaway, 10-11 Sari ONeal, p12c brackish_nz, p13rt lara-sh, 14b Cathy Keifer, 14c Cathy Keifer, 14r, Cathy Keifer, 15r Jacob Hamblin, 15l Cathy Keifer, 16t Laurie Barr, 16l Laurie Barr, 16b Laurie Barr, 16r Laurie Barr, 17t Laurie Barr, 19tl Leena Robinson, 19tr Leena Robinson, 19r Kate Besler, 19b Roman Pelesh, 22–23 Fizpok, 24t Jacob Hamblin, bcl Valentin Valkov, bcc ESB Professional, bcr Henrik Larsson

CONTENTS

WHAT IS A BUTTERFLY?

A butterfly is a type of **insect**. Insects have three pairs of legs, making six legs altogether.

The wings of a butterfly are covered in many tiny scales.

The scales are usually patterned and coloured.

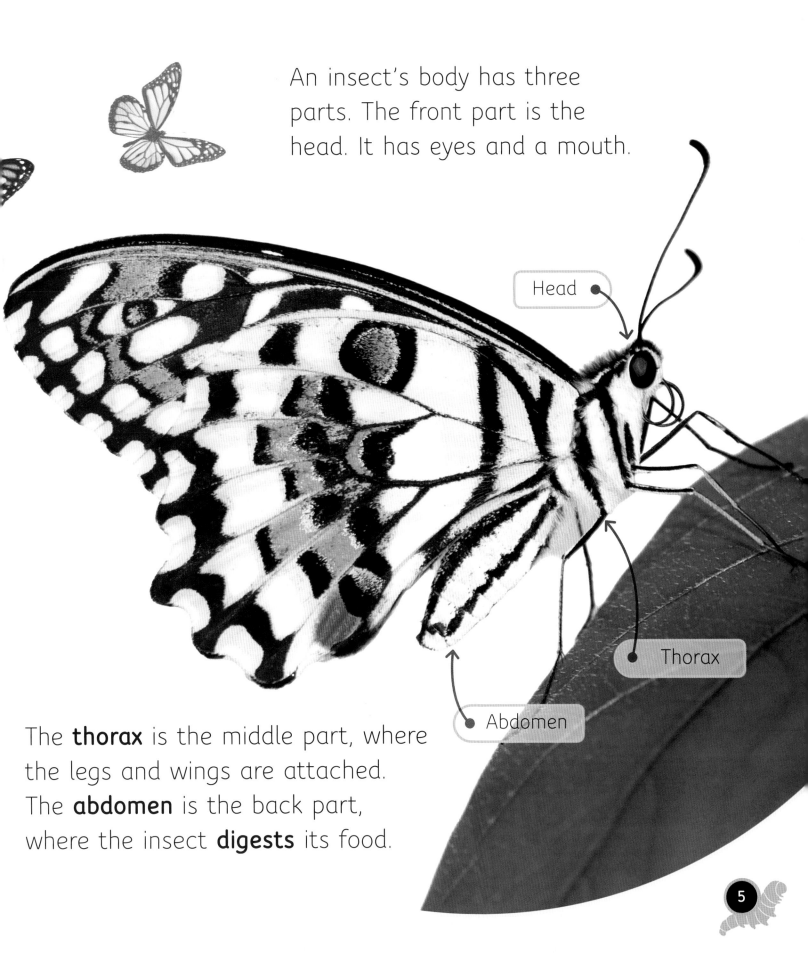

An insect's body has three parts. The front part is the head. It has eyes and a mouth.

Head

Thorax

Abdomen

The **thorax** is the middle part, where the legs and wings are attached. The **abdomen** is the back part, where the insect **digests** its food.

5

THE STORY OF A BUTTERFLY

A butterfly starts life as a little egg. It will hatch into a hungry caterpillar.

2

Caterpillar

A butterfly has four stages in its life cycle.

1

Egg

3

4

Pupa

Adult

The story of how an
egg grows into an
adult butterfly is
called a **life cycle**.

7

A New Life Begins

It is spring. A female butterfly is looking for a safe place to lay her eggs.

She lays them under the leaves, where they are hidden from view.

Monarch butterflies lay their eggs on milkweed plants. The eggs stick to the leaves.

Egg

Different types of butterfly lay their eggs on different plants. Peacock butterflies choose nettles. These plants have stinging hairs. The stings stop animals from eating the nettles and the eggs.

Nettles are a safe place for peacock butterflies to lay their eggs.

THE EGGS HATCH

A few days later, the eggs hatch, and a tiny yellow caterpillar comes out of each one.

Caterpillars spend most of their time eating, so they grow quickly.

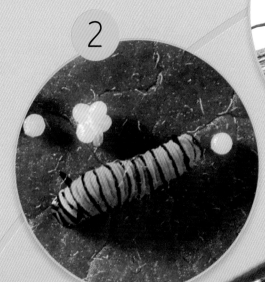

Monarch caterpillars become stripy as they grow older.

4

5

When a caterpillar moults, it wriggles out of its old skin.

A caterpillar is also known as a **larva**.

As a caterpillar grows, its skin becomes too tight, and splits. The caterpillar sheds its skin, revealing a new one underneath. This is called **moulting**.

STAYING ALIVE

A caterpillar is soft and juicy. Lots of other animals want to eat it, but there are some clever ways to stay alive!

The caterpillar's stripes warn hungry birds that it is poisonous.

A monarch caterpillar eats milkweed plants. The leaves are **poisonous**, and they make the caterpillar taste bad.

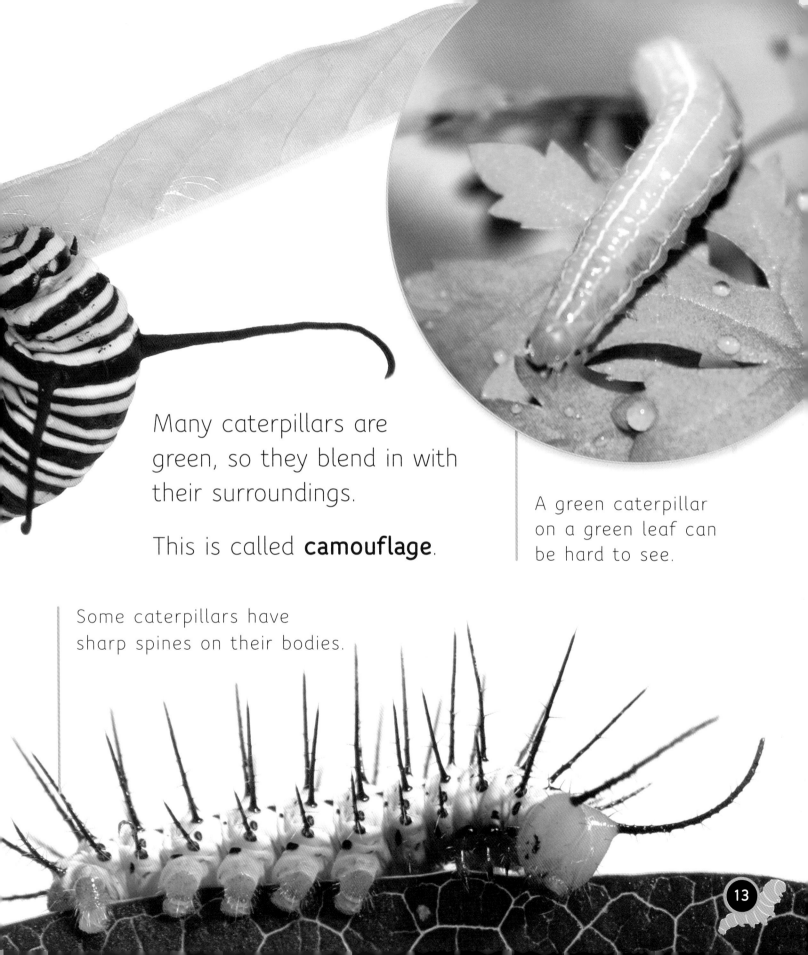

Many caterpillars are green, so they blend in with their surroundings.

This is called **camouflage**.

A green caterpillar on a green leaf can be hard to see.

Some caterpillars have sharp spines on their bodies.

MAKING A PUPA

Caterpillars grow fast. After about 14 days, a caterpillar is ready to change into a **pupa**. This is the next stage of its life cycle.

Once the skin is shed the pupa hardens.

It moults for one last time. The pupa is already formed under the caterpillar's skin.

A caterpillar makes a silk thread, and uses it to hang from a leaf.

14

4

The pupa is
tough on the
outside to
protect the
insect inside.

5

The caterpillar
begins to change
inside its pupa.

A pupa is often camouflaged.
It is green, brown or grey, and
hidden under a leaf.

A BUTTERFLY APPEARS

After two weeks the pupa turns dark. Something amazing is about to happen!

1

The orange wings of the butterfly can be seen inside.

2

The pupa cracks open.

3

The butterfly climbs out.

It sits on the empty pupa case.

4

Male's dark spot

It rests for
a few hours
before it
can fly.

6

An adult butterfly does not
grow any more. Male and
female monarchs look similar,
but males have small dark
spots on their back wings.

Then it spreads its
wings so they can dry.

5

BUTTERFLY LIFE

Butterflies flutter around, searching for food. They feed on sweet sugary **nectar** inside flowers.

Most adults live for just a few weeks.

It is mating time. Male butterflies stop looking for food. They look for females instead.

Once the butterflies have mated, the female lays her eggs. A new life cycle then begins.

A LONG JOURNEY

As the summer comes to an end, monarch butterflies start an amazing journey, called a **migration**.

They fly to warmer places. The journey can cover thousands of kilometres and takes more than two months.

Millions of monarch butterflies spend the winter resting on trees.

In spring, the butterflies set off to their summer homes. On the way, they mate. Their young change into butterflies and continue the journey.

The monarch butterflies wake up when warm weather arrives.

GLOSSARY

Abdomen
The back part of an insect's body.

Camouflage
Patterns and colours that help an animal to hide.

Digest
When food is digested, it is changed so the body can use it for energy. Animals need energy to live and to grow.

Insect
An animal with six legs and a body divided into three parts.

Larva
Another name for caterpillar.

Life cycle
The story of how a living thing changes from birth to death and how it produces young.

Migration
A long journey made by an animal or a group of animals.

Moulting
When an insect sheds, or gets rid of, its old skin.

Nectar
A sweet liquid made by flowers to attract insects to them.

Poisonous
Harmful to eat. Poison can kill living things.

Pupa
When a caterpillar changes into an adult butterfly.

Thorax
The part of an insect's body between the head and abdomen.

INDEX

NOTES FOR PARENTS AND TEACHERS

- Teach children how to keep safe while investigating animals and their life cycles. For example, they can be shown how to recognize plants and animals that sting, or are poisonous.

- Teach children how to observe animals and, if appropriate, handle them with care. They should observe animals in their natural environment, without disturbing them or their habitats.

- Ask the children to draw, colour and label the stages of a butterfly's life cycle.

- Visiting a wildlife garden or butterfly sanctuary helps children to understand the importance of habitats. Explain how habitats can provide shelter and food for lots of different animals and plants.

- Be prepared for questions about human life cycles. There are plenty of books that can help you to give age-appropriate explanations.

- Talking about a child's family helps them to link life processes to their own experience. Try drawing simple family trees, looking at family photo albums and sharing family stories.